Becoming a Positive Thinker

Patrick Uchechukwu

Becoming a Positive Thinker

First Published by Chiysonovelty International 2016

ISBN: 9785033724
ISBN-13: 978-9785033724

Chiysonovelty International
Plot 8 Evule Avenue
Aba,
Nigeria
Email: chiyson@minister.com
Phone: 234-909-227-1088

Printed in the United States of America

Thinking positive is a major step of becoming great.

CONTENTS

DEDICATION

I dedicate this book to God Almighty.

INTRODUCTION

In life, there are really no victims of poverty and hardship, but there are really victims of negativity. Men who have been enslaved by the world they created on the inside.

Every activity of man centers on his mind, and every activity of the mind determines what becomes of a man. Men become what they are if they think that is what they should be. Becoming a positive thinker will help you see things on a whole different phase of thinking.

Written in a deep inspiration and with less theory, *Becoming a Positive Thinker* is a practical and motivational work with clear connection on how you can restructure your mind and take control of your life. *Your mind controls your life.* Your mind is the mind that you have.

The mind is one of the greatest assets and enemy man has ever known. It has the power to create anything any man desires. There can never be greatness, fulfillment, achievement, success, career, legacy, impact, progress and wealth when the mind is in poverty. Becoming a positive thinker encompasses how to succeed with the mind and how to knock down the fear of failure.

What I can never guarantee is the total absence of negative thoughts, because they will always set in and what I can also never guarantee is your inability to remain and maintain a positive mind just as you are about to go through this book.

The greatest accident in life is not a motor accident or physical accident, but the accident of the heart.

Man: Pat I can't stop thinking

Pat: hahahahahaha

Man: why are you laughing over this issue?

Pat: I'm laughing because man can never stop thinking

Man: Ehh!

Pat: Yes, but what man thinks about makes a whole lot of difference.

Thinking is a natural endowment in man, but thinking positively is a personal development by man. Nonetheless, this rarely can be possessed by few.

"People who are unable to motivate themselves must be content with mediocrity, no matter how impressive their other talent."-
Andrew Carnegie

According to Carnegie, if you are not positive in mind forget about succeeding, no matter how talented you are.

Just like Mike Ditka noted *"the ones who wants to achieve and win championships motivate themselves."* Here, it is quite clear that talents become unutilized when the mind is undeveloped, dreams becomes unrealized when the mind doesn't see reality. It is said that success is the maximum utilization of the ability that you have. But the truth is that, there can never be maximum impacts, when you are at minimum in your mind.

The point is obvious, positive thinking is a major step of becoming great. What shall we say then? Shall we continue in negativity, that failure may abound? Shall we live with a purpose and die with a purpose? Shall we live the life of a mediocre? I believe you have the answer.

If thinking positively is the major step then any man who desires to be great, must first work on the way he thinks. Below are lists of great men and women, who through positive attitude impacted lives including mine: Caroline Buckee, Regina Duga, Tony Fadell, Bre Pettis, John Maxwell, Bill Gate, Rose Uchechukwu, Ben

Carson, Gabriel Elendu, Zig Zigglar, Bon Elebe, Robbert H. Schuller etc.

The reason for short-listing these names is to get a better picture of who a positive thinker can become. In the first page; I made it clear that thinking is a natural endowment, but thinking positively is mainly a personal achievement and sometimes congenital, anyway.

O yes! It is mainly a personal achievement, but the good thing, is that *you can actually achieve it.*

Becoming a positive thinker is not easy, but it is possible.

Becoming a positive a thinker is not something one can develop in a day. Becoming a positive thinker is never easy, but it is possible, and this largely depends on the aspirant.

The above short-listed individuals have really made a lot of impact in the lives of millions of people by their positive-thinking life. An amusing story about the benefits of staying positive comes from a great thinker, Bre Petits, a co-founder and CEO of Makerbot Industries. Bre spent seven years of his life as an art teacher in Seattle public schools in Washington where he found teaching fascinating. Bre heard about 3-D printer (*a machine reminiscent of the star Trek Replicator, something magical that can create objects out of thin air. It can print manufacturing prototypes, end user products, aircraft engine parts and even human organs using a person's own cell.*) but couldn't afford one, because of how costly it was. So he began to think about how to make one for himself and finally he succeeded.

In 2009, Bre and two of his friends raised some funds to establish Makerbot industry and began building primitive 3-D printers (*Bre Petits was not the first person to pioneer 3-D printing, but laid the foundation of a new industrial revolution in the world*). Their first model was made from ply wood, which was then almost new to people, so Bre often explains the concept to people, who would always look at him, scratch their heads but would finally make a demand for it. Today, Makerbot is a leading company in making desktop 3-D printers (*a more advanced type*) that sells for $ 2,000 to $ 3,000.

YOU CAN

Many do attribute success to something reserved for some people, but the truth is, no man is born with success, fame and influence. Great people earn success, fame and influence for themselves. Do you want to earn it? It is possible if you believe you can and work towards actualizing it. It is in your best interest to know that you are the one to create your success and make it a success. Just as Bre acknowledged that, *"When you are a thinker or a maker and you want something, you make it yourself."*

Most times people fail before giving something a trial, and thereby having little or no belief in succeeding. It is doubtful that you will get it at the first trial, and it is also doubtful that you wouldn't get it after much trial. If you fear the beginning, you might just die before the end.

Doubt doesn't exist, it is not real, it only seems real when we fail to act, but believe is real, you see it, feel it, it leads you to success and that's what makes it more real. For any man to succeed in anything, be it career, purpose, ambition, quest, marriage, relationship, education, ministry, etc, he must first succeed in creating a positive mind towards it. If it is not real, then make it real.

Positive thinking improves one's self-confidence.

Research has demonstrated that positive thinking can have wide varieties of benefit, from improving one's self confidence and psychological well-being to living a perfect and satisfied life. One can't effectively carry out a task that requires *"I-can"* mentality with an *"I-will try"* mentality. Have you ever wondered why some people after preparing perfectly behind the scene flops or fails to trap of stage freight? The reason is that they think that they don't worth doing that particular task.

It is not about the crowd or the personnel present at that particular time. The difference between an individual who performs effectively on the stage and one who doesn't is their *mind authenticity*. You have 99.9% excellent chances of succeeding and 99.9% chances of failing, but it depends on your 99.9% decisions.

"You are the only person on earth who can use your ability." - Zig Zigglar

NEGATIVE MIND, NEGATIVE ACTIONS

Most of the rebels and militant groups found around the world are as a result of manipulated minds by some persons, on the grounds of misguided grievances which leads to subsequent and unwholesome pogroms and attacks launched on governments and civilians. It is not what happened that led to these attacks, but what happened to the minds of those that carry out this attacks.

Some religious organizations prefer inculcating doctrines into the minds of their younger ones, at the tender age because they know when their minds are manipulated, they will be religiously crippled for the rest of their lives. *It is the mind, not the character.* If you will cripple your mind for success, then you stand the chance of tripling your chances of succeeding.

For you to change a man, you must first change the way he thinks.

THE FACTOR

A politician campaigning wins the favor of the masses when he creates a positive impression in the minds of the people with fascinating manifestoes and programmes. Employees in a company works perfectly and productively when the employer creates a positive working environment.

A football team performs wonderfully well when the coach motivates them, parents succeed in connecting with their children, when they always show positive parenting attitude towards them. A pastor or clergy reaches out to more people when he preaches and speaks more positive sermons to his congregation.

A positive mind is a great instrument in managing stress and effective performance. It is not how herculean the task or work is, but how positive you can stay. A positive mind is a relaxed mind.

"A positive thinking will let you do everything better than negative thinking will." - Zig Zigglar

POSITIVE THINKING, POSITIVE ACTION

Thinking positively or negatively influences our daily life, because there is a close connection between our character and what we always think, it either determines what we do at a particular time or at a future time.

In the Holy Scripture, a great light was shaded over the thought of man and its impact when it acknowledged in **Proverbs 23:7**, *"for as he thinketh in his heart, so is he..."* You can never hide your thought for it will surely reflect through your character. If you can't get there mentally, you can't get there physically. Thinking positively creates room for creativity, it gives room for development.

Ideas are like crops which when planted under a favorable condition, grow and bear fruits.

A positive mind is a condition required for the growth

9

of every good idea. Have you ever wondered how things are invented? How men invent things? It is very easy because they are positive thinkers. To be a positive thinker is to be able to see through things. Before the invention of things, no one has ever seen them work, not even the inventors, but they do believe that it would work and it works.

The secret to their succeeding is simple! They make it work in their minds first so that no matter how they fail, they would never stop trying because they have seen it work on their minds. No man is ever great by merely thinking but thinking positively and any man who fails to think positively will only be garbage where men dump their ideas.

To get extra-ordinary answers we must see and think beyond the ordinary.

IT'S IN YOU

CNN Presenter Michael Manisa noted *"the phones in our pockets and the web at our fingertips. The way we live, the way our children learn and the discoveries that make us excited about the days ahead. None materialized out of thin air. Great advances come from great thinkers."* Every man is created with numerous abilities and potentials, but few people know of these and only few are ready to make sacrifices for it. No wonder the world's dependent population both in First and Third worlds has escalated than normal and government of every country battles with the issues of job insecurity.

The world would be a better place, if men can change the way they think, from *"what they can offer"* to *"what I can offer them."* No man has ever given the world the best without giving himself the best and this begins with seeing things very different from the way every other person does.

There is no doubt that we all are gifted but what makes us what we actually become are the choices and decisions we make. Every decision and action we take has a way of contributing to our future and this defines what we want. Our gift and abilities matter a little, but what natters a lot is the decisions we make which affects our gift and determines what becomes of us.

How greatly gifted we are can never determine how great we become. A coach once commented about his player this way *"he is not one the most talented players but his attitude towards his development drives him beyond others."* This story will put you in a more positive perspective about who you are:

Brian Taylor a nine–years boy who rode his bike over a hundred miles and raised one hundred dollars for the America Cancer society was told by many that his dream of ever riding a bicycle was only a dream that can never be achieved owing to the fact that he had only one leg. That didn't stop Brian; rather he devised a way of riding the bicycle without falling. He put a scrap over the pedal of the bike to keep his foot fastened to it. Now he can ride like a pro. With this Brain rode miles and started developing an incredible height of agility and stability which gave him a world class achievement. Brian wasn't just like every other person who can ride the bike, none was he the most gifted but he was truly determined to get what he wanted, to do what he wanted and that shaped his life .If Brain was an option many would definitely not choose him and would have written him off "less human", of course, he was just not like every other human being but he achieved what "most human" couldn't achieve and that made him more than human.

Any good thing a man dreams positive has a way of influencing and positively impacting his life.

One of the most amazing thing about thinking positive is that it has the power to drive a man to a great length of achievement. Positive thinking initiates determination, dedication, commitment and above all everlasting joy towards anything any man is doing. There is so much you can achieve in this life when you think positively. You can set your mind to work positively and enjoy everlasting joy in the following area:

Career pursuit

Realization of one's potential

Building a great family

Managing an organization

Parenting

Academic pursuit

Connecting with one's employees

Maintaining a healthy relationship

Reaching out to one's congregation

Being a sales man

And living a fulfilled life

Brian's positive dedication did not just enabled him to do what he loved most, but also made him a point of reference for many, including me. He never invented any machine nor carried out any powerful surgery, did he? I do not think so! He only readied his mind for what he desired and got committed to it and that made so much difference. I see a Brian of his time, who through committed mind harnessed the little within for greater achievement in a distinctively different way.

"I believe life is constantly testing us for our level of commitment and life's greatest rewards are reserved for those who demonstrate a never-ending commitment to act until they achieve. This level of resolve can move mountains, but it must be constant and consistent. As simplistic as this may sound it is still the common denominator separating those who live their dreams from those who live in regret." - Anthony Robbins.

Show me a positive thinker and I will show you his greatness. Ben Carson's friend, Dolin Long once said *"learn everything you can, think yourself."* If one can't try to solve one's problem with the resources within, one will keep seeking for help and no matter the kind of help one gets one can never get satisfied.

AND THE STEPS

There is hope for any man who desires to be a positive thinker. I wrote initially, that becoming a positive thinker is never achieved in a day or instantaneously, so do not stop when you are not getting expected feed backs. Becoming a positive thinker can be developed or achieved with some steps when adhered to. Visually, it looks like this:

PRODUCTION

EMULATION

CONNECTION

MOTIVATION

Let's consider each steps:

Step 1: MOTIVATION

Most times, employees do complain about inability to deliver as expected, employers complain about the low performances of their employees, coaches being frustrated by the lackadaisical performance of their teams, government complaining of the ineffectiveness of their ministries after massive investments. Can you gaze what the problem is? Of course, the problem is lack of *motivation*.

A research conducted recently by Jamie Harter and Teresa Amabile, a co-author of the best-selling book *The*

Progress Principle, shows that over $300 billion is lost annually because of employee disengagement by their employers as a result of their ineffectiveness and inability to deliver. James Harter stated that business unit sales and profits at one point in time are predicted by employees feeling about the organization at earlier points in time. He once stated *"you will find it clear that happiness boost performance."*

No man, no matter how successful he is can live an effective life without motivation. Motivation can be one's spouse, departmental heads or managers in companies, the hope of a better future, one's team coach, one's parent, a mentor, a peer group, a friend, one's environment, a teacher, a clergy, the scripture, motivational books, salary (*seldom*).

I was motivated when writing this book by the hope of positively impacting lives in the world. Every man needs to be motivated, likewise every student, no matter how brilliant needs motivation. The imperfection of man exposes him to mistakes, discouragement, doubt, self-intimidation or inferiority complex, therefore needs motivation. Motivation is like an engine of a moving train with different parts, which converts power to motion.

No matter how you teach a man, direct a man, if you do not motivate him, the result will always be either too poor or average, but never excellent. Most times, students in high schools and colleges are often than less tagged *"dumb"* because of their inability to perform, but a little motivation from their instructor can go a long way to tell them that no one is ever perfect, but our commitment to things, task or academics can make a whole lot of difference regarding efficiency. Nothing can replace motivation not even skills. Motivation can be either negative or positive depending on the connection.

Step 2: CONNECTION

Every successful man always has a way to his success. America poet philosopher Raph Waldo Emerson said *"every man is a hero and oracle to somebody and to the person, whatever he says has an enhanced value."* Every man who desires to grow in positive thinking must always be connected to positivity or negativity must set in. The level of one's challenges was once some else's level of success. So if you want to progress in becoming a positive thinker, then you must be connected to something bigger than what is bigger than you.

No man is perfect, but with constant correction and

communication with a superior mind, a hero is forged.

Step 3: EMULATION

Emulation can happen from afar but to make emulation more productive, one has to emulate people one is connected with.

When you have successfully gotten to the step of connection, then you have successfully made a trail of great advancement for yourself. Do you know why a man who has lived his whole life in a slum is totally different from a man who did not? Do you know why people are different?

Have you figured it? At the early stage of every development in children, there are certain things that tends to glamorize their interest, whether negative or positive and these things go a long way in affecting their psychological and physiological development, when constantly exposed to it.

John C. Maxwell once noted *"no matter what you tell your children to do, their natural inclination is to follow what they see you doing."*

Most times we get influenced with things we see, associate with and somewhat trying to be like them and these lead to emulation. Emulation has the power to influence the way we live, dress, perceive things and react to situations. Emulation can happen from afar, but to make emulation more productive, one have to emulate people that one is connected with and not mostly public figures or celebrities, whom one never gets to relate with. Not every successful man or woman can be placed as a role model, and this is where people get things wrong. People tends to imitate and also do things the way most people who are celebrities do, and not trying to do it first, their way.

Many can be successful, but few can only suit your purpose and who you really want to be. Emulation when done wrongly can lead to limitation.

How can you get discouraged because you are not getting it rightly the way others or celebrities do, when you are different?

We always aspire to be like most celebrities and public figures, but have never tried to consider whether these people aspire to be like us. One can't emulate something or individual, one would never like to be addressed to as. Do you aspire to be like the person you are emulating or the position and social status you want to attain? I'm not trying to rule out emulation, but you have to understand that there are things that you have to work out your own way; no one can ever handle that for you.

To become a better positive thinker, you must always have a mindset, which mostly should come from who you are emulating; of course connected with. If the person is of an outstanding quality, then you have to emulate as many characters and life styles as possible. But you have to ask yourself this question, if he is not by my side or with me, can I do it effectively more than when he or she is? Can I live positively? Can I still live in line with what I want in life? Can I produce great results on my own? If yes, then it's time to advance to the next step, which is the production stage.

Step 4: PRODUCTION

Whenever I stand on the shoulders of great men, I become a consumer, but whenever I try to stand on my own, I become a producer.

Production is never complete until it gets to the consumer that it was intended for. Thinking positively and being a positive thinker are totally two different things. You can think positively for some intervals, and the next minutes you have lost it all, but being a positive thinker graduates to the stage of constantly staying positive in every situation. For one to reach this stage, one has to stop consuming and start producing for it is the only way to check whether you have successfully gone through the most three important stages of becoming a positive thinker.

An employer can positively produce a brand new set of employee who can work effectively and enthusiastically by eliminating words like *"is that what you are paid for?"* and using words like *"you can do better."* A teacher can positively produce a set of students who are not only scintillating, but promising, by encouraging them rather than making them feel different and not wanted. A coach can positively produce an invincible team by invigorating them with *"go words."* A salesman can break records by creating a positive public relationship by using optional and appealing words on his customers, rather than using imposing and compelling words, no matter how demanding and insatiable they can be, of course buyers are always right.

The production stage initiates self-confidence, resolves conflict and, win of people's trust and confidence. No man will ever wish to disappoint those that believe in him. *So it keeps one thinking positive.*

21

THEY COULD, YOU CAN

Now that you have a little view about becoming a positive thinker, it's now time for you to dig deep to becoming a positive thinker.

It is not that 'you' can't but that 'you' think 'you' can't – it has always been 'you.'

Everyone can comfortably point out his or her goals in life, but not everyone can live to achieve them. Benjamin Disraeli noted *"nurture great thoughts for you will never go higher than your thoughts."* Our greatness, goal and aspiration in life have a binding connection with our thought.

The true power of achievement lies in our mind and not in our physical strength or intellectual abilities; so when the mind is negative, the physical strength will be misused, intellectual abilities becomes inactive and purpose will be lost. So it all begins with the mind, of course, a positive one.

A Danish French philosopher noted *"man is a unique and isolated individual in an indifferent or hostile universe responsible for his own actions and free to choose his destiny."*

No man can run away from making a choice of destiny

in life; when one chooses to do nothing, one is making a choice and when one chooses to do something one is also making a choice. One thing is sure, the world wouldn't wait for any man. Howard Thurman put it *"don't ask, what the world need ask what makes you come alive and go do it. Because what the world needs are people who have come alive."*

One thing amazing about the world is, the world will keep existing and people leaving a good life, if you refuse to live up to who you are. The world can't know who we are if we don't tell them. Great men are not known because they once or are living on earth, but because they did something that made the world know that they once lived or are living; something that amazed the world, something that the world has never seen.

Don't wait until you invent an automobile or a robot before you start doing something. There is one thing wonderful about human beings; they have the power of doing something new and extraordinary. If you can't affect change on those around you, you can never affect change on the world. Jim Rohn illustrated it this way *"humans have the remarkable ability to get exactly what they must. But there is a difference between a "must" and "want."*

23

You can be someone that changes people's lives through your actions and character. You can be someone that heals broken hearts with your words, and one day people will live to tell your story, and that's how greatness starts. It all begins and ends with a positive mind, a mind that is always ready to start the task. Willis R. Whitney expressed his mind this way *"some men have thousands of reasons why they cannot do what they want to, when all they need is one reason why they can."* The reason is if you can't, you wouldn't, you wouldn't be what you want to be. If you are too big for the small task, then you are definitely too small for the big task. So, start something, forget how bad It looks

Often times, we trash our lives than we help it, and until we begin to help ourselves, we will never see help. Don't destroy those innovative thoughts, because you feel you should have done more than that. That's why Geoffrey Gabrino said *"the real contest is always between what you have done and what you are capable of doing."* Whenever you are after what you should have done, and not what you ought to do; you will end up doing nothing. One unique thing about you is that you will always be capable of doing something.

According to Gian Menotti Carlo *"hell begins on that day when God grants us a clear vision of all that we might have achieved, of all the gift we wasted, of all that we might have done that we did not do."* You will always be remembered by what you have done, so the early, the better. Commit yourself to every good task, for you will never tell, what you will be remembered for.

The truth is, if you have never thought of what you should have done, you will never be moved to do something, but thinking about it always or where you should be, will totally destroy things, for it will initiate fear, lack of confidence, and frustration. You didn't do what you should have done, and you will never do, if you remain that way.

Without failure, there can't be success and without *"I would have"* there wouldn't be *"I will"* and you can't keep thinking about your failure without failing again. When a man always thinks about the past, he will definitely loose the sight of the present. You can never right the wrongs of the past, but you can always make amends with the action of your present.

Don't forget that your past was once your present and your present will become your past. when you keep thinking about the past, you will keep living in the past and surely you will pass away with it. When one is not dealing with the present, there can't be future.

When men fail, they should never fail to try.

There is no other connection between your past, present and future, other than you. So you are your past, present and can only be your future. Don't expect wonders or a total turn around in time to come.

So have you heard people say *"don't worry in the future, I will do this, I will try, I will start doing it, my future is bright, my future can only be bright."* The truth is, you are the bright you expect to be attached to your future. The future is divided into two phases: the first phase which is *"now"* has to do with what you are doing now, the foundation you are laying; the second is *"tomorrow"* which is when you are to showcase what you have been doing. Tomorrow is when you will have to build and live in the house you laid it's foundation, and that is actually the results. And when one don't have anything to showcase, there is no future. Do not expect magic, or a new dawn, because what you give in determines what comes out and what comes out is totally the product of what you gave in. This applies to every man, whether successful or not.

A man without a background will always have his back on the ground. A man without a foundation will always have to suffer degradation.

How successful you are now can never be seen to be the best or a better future, but you have made a right choice. The future is something that continues every day and every moment counts, so do not expect that you are already there. A single action can throw you into your worst night mare. Albert Schweitber once acknowledged that *"the great secret of success is to go through life as a man who never get used to it."*

The 'behind the scene' of every greatness are determination, focus and positive thinking; on the 'scene' are success, glory and manifestation of hard work.

IT'S YOU AND POSITIVE THINKING

Not even God can solve the problem of a man, but his heart, whatever he thinks works for him. If he thinks *faith can*, then *God can*. Of course, that was what this writer had in mind when he writes *"what makes you "you" is created by your existence, your existence in turn is determined by your choices. Thus the responsibility for who you are lies with you."*

God can't control the ways of man, but his heart, whenever he gives negativity a chance in his life, then he will live by its dictates. The Holy Scripture acknowledged the importance of man's heart to living a better and impacting life when it instructed that we should keep it with all diligences for out of it are the issues of life. Every wise choice comes from a positive thought. Every day the activities of man are center on his heart, and his ability to think right, you are the one to determine the day.

The everyday life of a man is made blessed and promising; but his actions and reactions determine what becomes of it.

CHAPTER ONE

A Positive Thinker Needs

A MENTOR THAT ENLARGES

"Good afternoon sir.

Yeh, Pat, how has it been with you?

Fine sir

Sir, I want to do something remarkable before leaving the school, but I think it is too late.

Pat, I want you to understand that every second of the day is good for a new beginning. It does not matter when you start the task, but what matters is having realized that you ought to have started doing something.

But sir, what can I possibly start doing?

Pat, there are numerous of things that you can do as a student, but the problem is that you have not thought about it.

Pat, I want to charge you with the responsibility of sharing positive words with the entire school in the beginning of every week, can you do that?

Sir, how can I do that?

Pat, you can because within you are numerous of abilities you don't know about.

You can because it is in you.

You can because there is no limitation to what you or anybody else in the world can achieve in life.

But, first, you have to see yourself doing it before you can do it.

Go get yourself prepared, it's time to change the school

Sir, how are mine to prepare?

Pat, you know the way I speak and the way you feel when I speak?

Yes sir,

Speak and make me feel the same way you do feel."

This is a typical conversation between a mentor and the mentored or a person who desires to live positively and change things around him.

These were the exact conversation between me and my high school instructor, Mr. Gabriel, many years ago. Mr. Gabriel was my science instructor, who started planting the seed of greatness and positive thinking in me. He would always make us stay for a very long time on social programmes, to listen to his messages; he always titled *"Inspirational Dew."*

He is a man anybody can point out as a positive thinker, and that is why he is on the list I afore listed. He might not have gained a worldwide recognition. But he has built and raised great intellectuals. He is a builder, an enlarger. As he would always tell you, *"it does not matter what or who you are or who you are not, because you are something, whether "A" or "B."* He would tell me that great men are not remembered and known because of their fame, but what they did that brought them fame and recognition. I strongly believe that one day what he has been doing over the years will bring fame in due course.

He always told me to get committed to every good work that I am doing not because of its financial intake, but because of the Joy I would gain over it. He made those around him to understand that in every treasure, there is a value, so in order to get the value in every good thing we do; be it benevolent service to humanity or service to God, we should always treasure it.

In his best-selling book *Steps to Becoming a Phenomenon* he stated, *"clear your mind, look into your desire with your whole heart and you will see a purpose."* It is impossible to call him my god, but he has really enlarged my horizon toward life.

In his book, he writes *"Self-doubt is a serious disease of success. Self-doubt is really the great modern plague, but belief in one self can cure it. Doubt sees the obstacles, belief sees the way. Doubt see the dark, belief sees the light. Doubt sees limitation, belief sees infinity. Doubt questions, belief answers. you must lift up yourself beyond self-doubt."*

He has really planted an indelible print of mentorship in me.

The work of a mentor can never be substituted for anything in helping a person to becoming a positive thinker.

As Bill Gate put it *"everyone needs a teacher. It doesn't matter whether you are a basketball player, a tennis player, a gymnast or a bridge player."* Robbing mind with a superior mind can change one's life entirely. A mentor makes one see things differently. It is not easy to develop a positive mind without knowing the benefits in thinking positively. It is the work of a mentor to broaden a limited horizon.

To becoming a positive thinker, one must be a student.

A Positive Thinker is NURTURED

"good, good, good, good

Pat, that was a good sermon,

I really felt inspired.

That was really a great debut.

Pat, you have just gotten for yourself a ticket into the world of greatness. But Pat, whenever you speak try not to use lofty and compelling words on people."

"Good, good, good, good," as he would always say to complement you with a corresponding head that nodes back and forth.

Human beings are like assets, when you invest in them they appreciate, when you over use them or neglect them they depreciate and loose value. One of the ways to get people do something is to make them feel valued.

The *"good, good, good, good"* complement, one day got me thinking because he uses it even when I did it the wrong way. One day I asked him about the rationale behind it, because it was getting me confused, he told me that he can't build me positively by negatively destroying my little beginning with negative affirmation;

but can with correction and inculcation of positive words in me. He told me that he sometimes complements me not because I do get them right, but because I would have gotten them right if he had helped and showed me how.

Human beings are moved to be with people who they know will always get their backs if they fall, and growth is inevitable in such environment.

There is nothing that boosts one's confidence to doing something than belief and trust, people have in one.

If you assist people during their darkest hours, you will be their friends in the brightest hours.

There is nothing that triggers commitment, conviction and efforts on the part of a follower than being charged with a responsibility that gives recognition.

THEY SEE BEYOND DIFFICULTIES

"Paul: Pat, I want to be great

Pat: then you have to start doing something, because nobody becomes great by merely wishing for it. Paul but, people have done many things.

Pat: yes of course, but not everything."

This was a discussion between me and Paul a teenager that I mentored. In life, the level of one's knowledge on a particular thing determines one's level of belief on it.

And the eyes can never see possibilities when the mind thinks impossibilities so possibility first breeds in the mind before we see it.

Every great and bold step comes from a great conviction within.

CHAPTER TWO

A *Positive Thinker Must*

GET CONNECTED

"Motivation is what gets you started. Habit is what keeps you going." - Jim Rohn

Your habit to stay connected with whatsoever that keeps you motivated, keeps you. Negative thoughts are just like weeds that grow where and when not needed and plants can't perform well where they are. So they are constantly weeded. You have to constantly fight against them. What are I trying to say? The effective way to feed and train the mind positively is to give it a positive food. When your mind is constantly exposed to new positive ideas, it keeps becoming new.

To become a positive thinker, we must always aspire to be inspired or our minds will start expiring. Can you feel the differences between the texture of your palms and the sole of your feet, what do you observe? Which one is harder and which one seems soft? Of course, the sole of the feet is always harder than the palm. The sole of the feet tends to be constantly exposed to more roughness than the palm, thereby making it more rough, hard and strong. This is what happens to the mind when exposed to either negative or positive atmosphere. And when your mind is constantly exposed positively, it becomes stronger and gradually stable.

Just like Oliver Wendell Holmes noted *"man's mind-stretched by a new idea – never goes back to its original dimensions."* For one's mind to maintain consistency when it comes to positive thinking, it needs to be stretched. Stretched beyond its limit, beyond what it can stand, beyond negativity. A rubber band when expanded with the fingers remains the way we want it to be until when drawn together. This just explains what happens to the mind. The level of your mind positivity is as a result of your connection.

When we concentrate our strength in believing, we spend less time doubting. When we spend less time being afraid, we spend more time encouraging ourselves. When you spend more time in helping your life, you will spend less time in criticizing and trashing it. When you spend more time in thinking positively, you spend less time in negativity. This motivation like aforementioned can be your mentor, motivational book, seminars, inspiring words and every other positive minded personality around. In my whole life, I have never been defeated, because I have never stopped fighting and nothing have defeated my hope. You can never loose when trying, and when your hope is alive, you can never be defeated even in the face of defeat – that's the secret! Keep the dream alive and it will come alive.

"You can code your mind to think like a winner which is the first and most important step in becoming newer." - Zig Zigglar.

"Motivation is a fire from within, if someone else tries to light that fire under you, chances are it will burn you briefly."

It is just the best, self-motivation. You will always have to see the reasons to continue even when there are reasons to quit. You must be able to challenge challenges and this begins with knowing how to do them.

According to Paw Brown, *"the baby rises to its feet, takes a step is overcome with triumph and Joy – and falls flat on its face. It is a pattern for all that is to come. But learn from bewildered baby-lurch to your feet again. You will make the sofa in the end."* One day you will have to produce on your own so you need to emulate and develop how thing are defeated. You can't remain a baby. You really have to stand on your feet and the take the first step.

THEY KNOW WHAT IS RIGHT AND WHEN TO LET GO

Like John C. Maxwell and Jim Dornan clearly pointed out in their book *Becoming A Person of Influence*, "*If you nurture others but allow them to become dependent on you, you are really hurting them, not helping them.*"

To Measure your level of positivity, you really have to start trying things and facing challenges yourself, but not disconnecting completely from your mentor. One of the greatest advices one can ever receive is the advice one gives oneself. Because it calls for more personal discipline and adherence than we received from another source. Sometimes one needs to take a step than receiving courageous advices. A mentor plays some of the roles in transforming one into a positive thinker, but not all the roles.

One's success in life depends on many things but largely on one. If you receive all the advices as possible without working on yourself, you will end up wondering on past mistakes. Becoming a positive thinker is largely something that begins within. In other to live a problem-free life, one has to live a solution-life. So most of the work is *"you"* and only *"you."* We all have a way of dealing with our problems and when we fail to deal with it, we might end up living with it.

"The best motivation is self-motivation. The guy says "I wish one would come by and turn me on." What if they don't show up? You have got to have a better plan for your life." - Jim Rohn

CHAPTER THREE

A *Positive Thinker Has*

A WORK TO DO

"It is the use for which you put your mind that makes the world to mind you." - David Oyedepo

A mentor can teach, a mentor can direct, a mentor can give a new strength, a mentor can see the bigger picture, but a mentor can never think for you. That is why Marcel Proust put it this way *"The real voyage of discovery consist not in seeking new land scapes, but in having new eyes."*

Keep searching, there is always a way out. Do you think that God created you just to exercise the creation power or he created you just because it is his duty?

Everything that exists, God gave it a purpose. God can only give you a purpose, and you can only find out what it is. Do you know why people are born in poverty and also die in poverty or why people die without doing something outstanding?

It is because they never realized their purpose in life, and that should tell you more that God can never do that for you or any other person. Most times, people know their purpose in life, but die only knowing it and not living up to it. You know what you want, you know how you want it, but you don't know how to get.

Within us lies the power of knowing our purpose in life, the revelation of our self, do you know why? It is because you were programmed like that.

In the Scriptures, it is recorded that Adam gave names to the animals that we see today. God never did it for him, he never told him what to call them, and Adam had never being on earth before, but he did it, because the power to do it was within him. He never studied in any College to become a zoologist, but he is one of greatest zoologist the world has ever known. If the power was in Adam, then, it's in you.

Thinking positively is not something you need to go to school for, is something you need to develop and not acquire, because it is within you. Many people go to world-class schools, but live at the mercies of those who never saw the four walls of a school.

One of the greatest achievements in life is not building a mansion or owning a trillion-worth of company, but developing a positive mind.

Yes, when the mind is crippled wealth is misused, purposes are unrealized, and life becomes empty. You can create wealth for people, but live in internal poverty. My friend in the world of great thinkers, Myles Munroe once told a story in his best-selling books *In Pursuit of Purpose* about one of the richest men in America who wanted to take his life because he found out his life was empty, regardless of his wealth and fame.

"The initiative mind is a sacred gift and rational mind is a faithful servant." - Albert Einstein

It is a gift given to us by God, and that is why he instructed for proper guidance over it.

You see, it is not God; it is you not your environment, not your society, not even the devil. A rational thinking will always be a faithful servant and always at your service, if only you can develop it. You still have it, because God gave it to you. But are you willing to accept it? Often times, people pray for helpers but are myopic to see them.

Is it that you don't see helpers or you don't have the eyes to see them?

Do you know why many pray and seem not to get

answers, the more people ask the less it seems they receive, is because they don't even know what God has given it to them or when He has answered their prayers. It can be in form of inspiration that will boost you to greatness, a local friend you never valued.

We love *"already made"* and do not to produce them ourselves. How can you ask for wealth and greatness when you haven't even developed the little gift you have? You don't get, not because God doesn't give but because you can't even see.

Until you retrieve that which is yours, you will never get that which you want. There is no magic about this, God didn't make you different for making sake or give you those gifts for giving sake, but he programmed it as a channel for his blessing. Is it possible for a farmer who prays everyday for a great harvest without sowing a seed to have a bountiful harvest?

God can only make it prosper if you do it proper.

Most people take the right decision, but stand on the wrong direction, thereby receiving the unpredicted. That is, gift is a channel for his blessing, if only you can develop it and use it, you will become great; it begins with a positive mind. Just like novelist Robert Louis

Stevenson rightfully stated it *"Don't judge each day by the harvest you reap but by the seeds you planted."*

There is no mystery about it. How you understand life determines how you live it and how you live it determines how you end it.

The universe is not complete, because some people refused to contribute to its completion. Many have failed to live up to their potentials in order to contribute, thereby depending on what others has contributed.

Just like those that God purposed to lead and harness a nation's resources most times end up diverting it to private satisfaction and others go enslaved to poverty.

Many have existed and gotten into extinction, while others has lived and gotten to their destination. Wow! It will surprise you how Oscar Willde stated it *"To live is the rarest thing in the world, most people exist that is all."*

Those who live and those who exist are not the same. Let us explore the difference between those who live and those who exist.

The following are the differences between those that live and those that exist:

Those that live change things	Those that exist accept things.
Those that live, leave the world empty.	Those that exist leave the world filled up.
Those that live, live for a purpose.	Those that exist die with a purpose.
Those that live, live even when they are dead.	Those that exist, die even when they are alive.
Those that live, live the life of legacy.	Those that exist, exist for emergency.
Those that live, are the source of creativity.	Those that exist are dump for creativity.
Those that live, live for others.	Those that exist, exist for themselves.
Those that live, live the life of nobody.	Those that exist, exist for the life of somebody.
Those that live, live a fulfilled life.	Those that exist, exist for a dream filled life.
Those that live, live to dominate.	Those that exist, exist to populate.
Those that live, skip excuses.	Those that exist, give excuses.

Those that live, live fail and try.	Those that exist fear to try.

Reviewing the difference above, you will notice that there are men who live when they are dead, and there are men who are dead when they are alive. There are those who left an indelible print on the epoch while they were alive and can never be wiped out in all generation to come. So they live even when they are dead.

It is within the power of God to show us what we don't know about ourselves, but within our power to show the world what they don't know about us.

May be you already know about it, but you haven't created the environment for it to manifest. Start developing the positive environment filled with positive atmosphere, begin with emptying your mind of negative thoughts, for it will never thrive when surrounded by enemies. My mentor will always remind me to build my ideal world where I dwell and where things exist at my permission.

Myles Munroe in his best-selling book *Pursuit of Purpose* underscored it this way *"He's (God) much more concerned with the attitudes of your heart than the environment or condition in which you live."* A man bequeathed with estates of wealth, but with an undeveloped mentality can be likened to a gate warden who looks after his master's mansion when he is away and never gets to build one. Life is beautiful and everyone can live a beautiful life; It all begins with thinking positively.

CHAPTER FOUR

The Inevitable

Nature will one day query you about the contribution you failed to make just as it queried this man in this story below which was written many years ago.

There was a man who was born in a particular village. He grew up in that same village with his friends who were successful. He married and managed to raise up a small family in his late father's old brick house. One day as he was walking down the street with his son for sightseeing, he began narrating to his son about the history of the village. He pointed out to his son all the houses built by friends and brothers. When they finally got home, his son asked him *"father, we went out for sightseeing and it was really thrilling, you told me the history of the village and how the houses were built by your friends and brothers but you never showed me yours."* The father looked at him, laid on the couch, and wept.

Just like the way everyman can point out the successes of others, but few can point their own success. Your generation will demand for your success and fulfillment, they will ask you questions that will stare you in the face and demand answers. Let look at the way Abraham Lincoln put it *"And in the end, it's not the years in your life that counts, it's the life in your years."* Of course it is possible for you to live a life filled with vacuums. Many have lived years on earth and not life on earth, and one of the funniest things about their lives is, no matter how they wanted to live a selfish life, a life that doesn't contribute, in one way or the other they answered questions for it. Do you know the reason why ? Their lives are one way or the other connected with other people's lives just like yours connects with other peoples.

When a man fails, he not only failed himself but his generations because there are countless number of people who directly or indirectly would have benefited from him.

There are people you represent, there are people who look up to you, there are people who believe in you. What do they get? Disappointment and frustration or hope and joy. You have to understand that you didn't just fell from the sky; something brought you here for a purpose, your existence is unique and it will be a sin against God, humanity, me and yourself, if you fail to deliver.

A few minutes mistake that you make today can throw you forever into your world of frustration tomorrow. Start out on something, discover new lands, try out new methods, defile traditions, break rituals and remember Its no obligatory that it must pay off today, but it will definitely pay off someday.

It is better for me to suffer while bending my back today and forever straight it tomorrow, than to straight it today and forever bend it tomorrow.

It is better you plant the seed today and wait for the harvest tomorrow than planting no seed at all, of course the bigger the seed the bigger the harvest.

BEYOUND DREAMS AND PROBLEMS

If the achievement of success or greatness in life was just by dreaming, then everybody would be great. But life is where men who desire to be great wakes up from their dreams and fight for the actualization of their dreams.

O yes? It doesn't end at dreaming, there is more to it! In the scriptures, it was written that Joseph dreamed and worked towards it not sleeping over it. If you have seen it, go for it.

I once heard a man say *"I shall return."* There is no other time than now. You really have to understand that there is always plenty of reasons to do the wrong things and always plenty of reasons to do the right things, but most times, we look at the wrong reasons and end up in problems. You can always make the right decisions if you want or give excuses. When a man fails to make a decision that will build his life, then the next thing will be to cause a destruction that will collapse his life.

When a man fears to fail, he fails more than he feared.

You can't run away from problems without meeting problems, because life itself is full of problems and the easiest way to live a problem-free life is to live a solution life.

One thing is always sure, every problem has a solution. It existed from something and it will take something to extinct it.

Every problem exposes a solution.

The bigger your doubt grows the bigger your problems, and the bigger your belief, the bigger your solution.

Live everyday as if you are dying tomorrow, with this at the back of your mind you will exploit every opportunity and be fulfilled. Just as Less Brown acknowledged *"In everyday, we have 1,440 minutes. That means we have 1,440 daily opportunities to make a positive impact."*

One funny thing about life; is if you fail to change things, things wouldn't fail to change you. Accept responsibilities for who you are for life mostly depends on responsibilities. The more responsibilities you handle the more ability you gain. Convince the mind of what you want, accept the responsibility that comes with and give all it takes.

Most successful people whenever they are asked about the secret of their success will always say that they knew what they wanted and what it takes to achieve what they wanted and they went for it with all determination and passion. But funny enough they always forget one factor and that is *"the mind factor."* The mind sets the mentality into motion and the mentality determines what the action to be taken, which in return brings success.

When the mind is not in order, there wouldn't be any passion, desire and determination. Every other thing will be engulfed by fear, doubt and weakness. Most of the things we do begins within conviction and whenever the heart is convinced, they mentality gets influenced. So you have to convince the mind.

Whenever the mind is convinced the eyes sees possibilities.

BEING THE BEST YOU CAN'T BE

If you don't care about the things people entrust in your care, people will never care to entrust things in your care. If you don't care about what God placed in your hand he will never care to place more in your care because he will knows that you will not care for it.

I believe if people look at what they are not, they can become what they want to be.

Our generation has lived beyond the age, when people are told to be the best they can be. This is a new age when people are expected to be what they can't be.

Of course your *"best"* can be anything, but what you *"can't be"* goes beyond that and it places a bigger picture. Don't get it all wrong, most people would believe that they are no match to some challenges and task therefore settling for what they can be able to achieve at ease and celebrate it their *"best."* What if they had done more, what if they hadn't settled for what they could just achieve. Mary Kay Ash gave it a good summary *"Don't limit yourself. Many people limit themselves to what they think they can do. You can go as your mind lets you. What you believe, remember you can achieve."* Don't stop there because most successful are there, or because you struggled to get there. Always plan to advance to another stage.

"To discover new lands, we must consent to live the sight of the shore." - Andre Glde

Some men discover shores, while some discover new lands. Awesome! George Benard Shaw concluded it when he said *"You see things and you say "why" but, I dream things that never were and say "why not."*

You can't quit or relax on the track, because you have gone far on it.

We can't afford to stick to the old things that were created by somebody we can't afford to keep managing them, so we must create something, something that others can use. It's now or never; yes that what it is. Begin that task or you die not doing it. Do you forget, there is always a reason for postponing it.

Marce Beynon Ray made it clear when he noted, *"Begin doing what you want to do now. We are not living in eternity.*

We have only this moment, sparkling like a star in our hand – and melting like a snowflake. Let use it before it is too late."

Am sorry it has to be you, but you can't change it. Whatever you have in you, the universe needs it, I need it.

FOR YOU TO BE GREAT, YOU MUST REGRET

O yes! You must regret for not going out for night parties, rather you chose to stay back to think out new ideas. Yes you must regret for not going out with your friends to catch fun and pleasure, rather you sit in that lonely corner going through books for knowledge. You must regret and pay the price of not sleeping overnight rather you decided to experiment on the new ideas. Yes, you must regret for not settling for the pleasure you wanted so dearly.

I call these regrets, good regret. It is a temporal regret for permanent greatness. Do not fail to do it because you wouldn't fail to cry for it.

"I shall pass through life but once any good therefore that I can do, or any kindness I can show, let me do it now let me not deter or neglect it for I shall never pass this way again."

Do it, do it either right or wrong; the most important is

that you are doing something. Life without experience is full of mistakes. The more mistakes you incur the more experience you gain and it contributes to your success.

According to Dohlin Long *"there is value in the wrong way of doing things.*

The knowledge gained from errors contributes to our knowledge base." So you see, it is not wrong that you did it the wrong way.

If you can't fly, run if you can't run, walk if you can't walk, crawl, but don't just stop doing something.

MOST SOLUTIONS WE GET COMES FROM THE DECISIONS WE MAKE

I have analyzed life, and I found out that life is one of the easiest thing ever; is the easiest because it has only one rule, which is *"DO THE RIGHT THING."*

Do the right thing and you will succeed.

Do the right thing and you fulfill your purpose in life.

Do the right thing and nature will not query you.

Do the right thing and people will believe in you.

Do the right thing and God will never withhold that

which is yours. Do the right thing and not even the devil can stop you.

Do the right thing and stand a chance to live forever.

Do the right thing and you will be remembered.

Do the right thinking and get the right result.

Do the right thing at the right time and you wouldn't have to suffer for clash of priorities that emanates from misplacement of priorities. Take the right decision and you wouldn't have to suffer from difficulties.

Do the right thing and nature will vindicate you.

Do the right thing and not what you think to be right.

"Just because you don't see solutions to problem do not give you the right to take the wrong decision." - Robert .H. Schuller

The above statement is a command. The solution to your success that you are searching for is the problem that you failed to solve and you never get the solutions unless you solve it.

A man certain about his destination can never worry about how long the journey will take provided he is moving towards that destination. Don't take hasty decisions because things seem not to be moving fine.

If being great was all about struggling then, most African countries would be the most developed.

You don't have to struggle life out of your life because you just want to make it or do things for its temporal needs. Of course, life calls for more than struggling. It calls for using our minds positively. With the mind you can create your world, with our minds we can in an hour do what ten men will do in two weeks. By using our minds positively we do achieve more, grow great, struggle less and do the right thing.

CHAPTER FIVE

The Access

"The greatest discovery of my generation is that human beings by changing the inner attitudes of their minds can change the outer aspects of their lives." - William James (*1842 – 1960*)

Your mind is one of your greatest instruments of achievements; no man can make it through life if his mind is not in order. No man has ever achieved greatness with the wrong character.

Look at a man who is truly fulfilled and a man who is struggling with life. What do you see? The truth is that both of them may look alike but their minds over the years have proven to differentiate them. Their minds have placed them in different positions in life and their minds have determined their heights of fulfillment.

There is no Joy in life that is more than the Joy that comes from the fulfillment of purpose, and nothing makes a man happy than to look at himself in the mirror every morning and find out that he is fulfilled.

In life, things becomes what they are to us depending on how we look at them and what we think they are. Just like success or fail is not reserved specially for any man, they just naturally come to us depending on the decisions and actions we take. Anything can yield success or failure to any man depending on how he handles it. So, it is possible for me to succeed in a task and another man fails in it. It all depends on how we look at things and react to it.

This explains the reason most of the things people look down on are the things that would have taken them to a great heights. Within every man lies his visa to the world of greatness and that is your talent which gives you an access. No man is born great, but there are just men who made use of what they have, and that is what made them great. That means, when we use what we have, we get what we want.

It is tragic that most of the problems men suffer are caused by men. And only man can solve them because they were created by him. Take a good study of your life, try to analyze the problems you have gone through and the challenges you are going through at the moment. You may try to find out how the problems came into being and who caused the problems. Most problems exist because we have refused to employ what would have naturally solved them. The easiest way to cause big problems in your life is by running away from the small ones, and that begins from blaming it on someone or something.

Just like one of the President of American, Eleanor Roosevelt explained *"No one can make you feel inferior without your consent."* It is in your best interest to know that no problem can gain access into your life if you do not have access to it, and the easiest way to gain access to problems is by dominating its property – fear. Fear of overcoming it, and when you fear to overcome it, it dominates to conquer you.

You are not God, so even the courage in you needs encouragement and the doubts in you need to be doubted. Of course, it is said that courage is not the absence of fear. If that be the case, then fear can be used to gain access to courage, if both exist together. Whenever you are in doubt, the power of courage is somewhere around the corner. To put this clearer, none of all these things ever existed, we create the fear we fear and most times we conclude about things, when things have not concluded about us.

Let us imagine it, when you feel positive about something and it turns out to be the opposite. How do you feel? Dejected or partially encouraged? If dejected or partially encouraged, then what explains why you were totally positive initially, what explains why you are feeling so bad afterwards? Let's look at it from a different view, when you feel so negative about something then it turns out well. How do you feel? How do you think?

We react to things based on situations and not how we naturally should feel. We create out the fear and doubt based on what we think, feel, see and believe and not how we should feel. That means, things determine what we think, how we feel, believe and naturally behave.

If this is possible, then you can reverse how you see, what you think and the way you behave. You can actually make things right when they seem bad, you can make things possible when they look impossible; you can feel important when you are rejected

Is it that it is difficult or it looks difficult?

When we expose our weakness, we make things difficult for ourselves, thereby implanting fear into our being and making thing appear more difficult than it seems. Fear is in the head, doubt is in the mind and courage is in our action. The truth is, doubt will always exist when you create it, but it will never increase if you don't increase it. It is very ridiculous to know that the things man fear are the things they would strangle if they were human beings.

Can't you see? It's trying to hold you there, whenever you want to go, it increases, but when you relax it decreases. Now get the strength, you would have never been here (*your current level of achievement*) if you have never thought you could, and you will never get there (*the next great level of achievement*) if you think you can't.

No time is ever special, unless the one we deem or see to be special. Just imagine that you want to organize a birthday party, you will invite friends and organize things to make it special. So you see it's you and your mind, not you and doubt or fear. It is not always easy, but it is always possible. I don't know fear, I don't know doubt, I don't know courage but I know myself – mind, that I can create them, so it works on my mind.

I am not afraid of what I am or what I can become, because I know what I can be if I want

IT'S YOUR DOING

In life, it is either you fight for what you want or you settle for what you don't want. It is either you fight for greatness or you settle for the ordinary. It is either you fight for success or you settle for failure. It is either you fight for what you really want or people will give you what they have.

According to my friend Jim Rohn *"Either you run the day or the day runs you."* Yes you! It is either you release what you have or what you have will die in you.

"if you are not willing to risk the unusual, you will have to settle for the ordinary." - Jim Rohn

You can't hide or run from being hurt by problems, challenges, temptation and trepidations of life without hurting yourself the most. You can't fear to fail by remaining on a particular stage of success.

The propinquity to success is the propinquity to failure. That one is succeeding doesn't mean that one can't fail and when you are near to success, you are more nearer to failure, because the higher you go, the tougher it becomes. When you stop climbing you dash into pieces because you have climbed up to great height. And the higher the height the greater the crash.

Success is not the ability to do it right but the consciousness of failure. Yes, failure is part of success, but fail for the good reasons not as a result of negligence.

I don't like failing, that is why I do everything possible to continue on the success track and that is a good mentality. When one fail for the good reason and tries again, one will rise to the utmost. But when one fail as a result of *"I have gotten there."* Hahahaha! One will definitely suffer and be dealt by failure. Well if you try, you might rise again. It is good for me to put it clear to you for a coherent understanding.

Men raise and fail, fail and raise, yeah this is normal, but better when for a good reason. Sometimes when men who failed or suffered a problem resulting from their bad life style, succeed and turn out a new life, there are many things they will have to live with and that is what I call the *"scare."* When a great wound heals, its pains will cease, blood will stop gushing out. Every other thing might evaporate, but something might remain immutable, and that is the scare of the wound.

When I was a kid, I mistakenly stormed the second toe in my right foot on a stone. I ran to mum and she helped me with it and for some time it healed. New tissues showed up, but there is something about this work that remained unchanged up to this day and that is the scare. Some people suffer the scare of guilt for contributing to people's failure, scare of being told about it. As unappealing as it might appear, I believe we still need to talk about it. The deepness of the wound determines the deepness of the scare. I am sorry but that is the reason we all need to maintain a nice life pattern. A person whose fingers were cut short because of crime can never have such fingers back even when he repents, except if there is God's intervention and that is peculiar.

NOW THE WAY OUT

My toes up till today is still black and I always feel bad about it. Nonetheless, whenever I look at it, it keeps telling me that if I literally diverge the wrong way, I might sustain more scares, and that has helped to keep me on the right track. So, let your scare take you to your star and not to the dark, for there is something darker in the dark.

Having a scare in life does not mean you should stop; rather it means you should good attempts to strive. I once told a man that there are some people no matter how you try to change them, you can never change them and there are some sins that lead to righteousness.

So who knows whether without that scare you will have never been the star. There is always a reason for a fall, perhaps to bend you to see what you can't see while standing. It is time for you to stand on your scare and see the star.

CHAPTER SIX

Your Mind,

Your Achievement

What you see is what you will achieve, and what you can't achieve, you haven't seen it. The only way to see it is by thinking about it with the eyes of your mind so that it will become visible and clearer to you. If what you think determines what you see and what you achieve, then you need to think more and see more in order to achieve more.

YOUR BEST AND THE NEXT

The level of your achievement was once someone else's level of under development, why try to remain there?

Nobody can be the best, but people can try what they call their best. If you think you are the best, in what you are doing, do not be surprised that people will rise, take it to the next level and even tell you more about it. One can be outstanding no doubt, but there is always a next step to one's best and that makes one's best actually not the best. To rephrase this, it actually makes you not the best

Don't compare yourself with things you have defeated, but

with things you are yet to defeat.

Most times people fear not because of the unknown but the known. Are you afraid of being there? The fact is people have been there. And there is always another step in every pursuit in life.

"For most people are not what they are that hold them back, but what they think they are not." - John Maxwell

You can never be what you are not, if you don't try to be it.

If you don't get used to a particular stage of success, you will get used to moving to the next, and when you get to a level without taking the next step you might as well go back to the first. Albert Schweitzer asserted it this way *"great secret of success is to go through life as man who never gets used up."*

THE SUCCESS TEST

Without challenges and problem people will never fail and challenges are on the way to the top not to stop people from getting to the top, but to know those which really want to get to the top; those who really know where they are going to.

If you don't know where you are going to, you might be going to where you don't know. Failures and challenges know that not everybody knows where they are going to, so they are there to stop those who want to get to the top but don't want to stand up to it. They are there because they know that the top is not meant for everybody. The top is meant for those who wants to pay the top price, those who can give it all there best. If doubt is stopping you from going to the top, then you have to fight the fight of doubt without doubting.

Always dream higher, think higher, aim higher, fight stronger, work harder, pray harder, you will definitely, go higher...

SETTLING FOR MORE

You don't have to accept things the way they are. You don't have to be going for the less, settling for the less and being among the rest. Just like someone noted *"if you don't like a thing, change it you are not a tree."* People see things the way it appears, thereby living their lives the way it is. If it must be somehow it must be good, it must not be odd even if you are not the best, at least you must be good at something.

"Everyman is a hero and an oracle to somebody." – Ralph Emerson Waldo

If you are not the moon, be the star at least the two shines; therefore let your strength be bigger than your weakness, your courage bigger than your fear, your answers bigger than your questions, your solutions bigger than your problems, your Yes bigger than your No, your success than failures and your fulfillment bigger than your success.

THE STRENGTH OF SUCCESS

Life without problems is a life prone to an unknown destruction. Things that make up a fulfilled life are success and failure. Whenever there is a problem, there is a way, and it is going to make a way. If problem brings more growth, then every man needs problem.

Robert H. Schuller stated it this way *"It is a problem when you don't have a problem."* The difference between a fulfilled man and a failure is that a fulfilled man looks for problem while a failure runs away from it.

What gave a man success gave another failure. Do you want to be fulfilled and successful in life? Then start looking for problems. It might look awkward, but that is just the strength of success. Don't forget more problems, more strength and more success.

CHAPTER SEVEN

The Successful
Mind of Discovery

Your success in life depends on your success in mind.

I can never be a failure in life, because I always succeed in my mind. You can never fail in the mind and succeed outside or succeed in the mind and fail outside.

Every success, discovering and fulfillment starts from the mind and what our mind looks like determines what our life will look like. What you discover in your mind determines what you go for in life.

Until you discover your niche in the world of greatness, you can never make an inch into your world of fulfillment.

The world is too big to contain whatever that will become of your potential when exploited, if not you wouldn't have been here. We don't live to survival, we don't live to sustain life, we live to multiply and live a fulfilled life. There is no spare life so enjoy it.

Many have lived what I call *"Let's survive stages of life."* They went to school, got a nice job, hired an apartment, got married, raised few children and live to see them grow to go through the same *"let's survive stages of life."* Many people live their lives emulating every other person; they take life as what it should be and suffer like others. Our lives appear the way they are now in view of the fact that we accepted to live that way. That is how we chose to live, how we chose to exist. When our lives become what it shouldn't be, it will become a problem and this problem affects our mind.

Most people are suffering from cancer of the mind. Let us re-think about the way we see life and definitely the way we live will change. You are meant for something and something is meant for you. It is wrong to think that you must become an envied person. Most people don't live to live a fulfilled life, they live to add value to their lives.

EARLY DISCOVERY

Some people are direction while some are just destination

If "*A*" needs to help "*B*" to get to "*Z*" then without "*A*," "*B*" can never get to "*Z*" and without "*B*," "*A*" the purpose is worthless. This is what our life just looks like.

Most times, we try to be like others, while others will try

to be like us. They desire to be like us and we don't even know it. Many lived and struggled for the right purpose, but in the wrong location. Most times, we are what we shouldn't be, but desire to be what we should be, thereby, being what we shouldn't be. Until all these things are in the right place, you might never get to the right place.

Discover it early and enjoy it early.

Many discovered it early and enjoyed it early, while others discovered it late and ended up not enjoying it.

This amazing but frustrating story will tell you what will happen if you don't discover it early.

This story is about a man who worked in his early stage of life as a hire-purchase truck driver. In his early thirties, he always wished and prayed to God to have his own truck and had always wished to have *"God's time is the best"* inscribed on it.

Unfortunately, he was unable to get it until his late eighties. Being so weak, frustrated and unable to continue with the job, he miserably inscribed *"God's time"* on it instead of *"God's time is the best,"* which was his initial intention. That's not where it ended. He rented out the new truck on a hire-purchase bases to a young fellow who started the way he started out many years ago.

Few years later, the young man returned his truck to him. Being so surprised, he imagined what the problem might be but little did he found out that the young man had acquired his own truck.

What happened? Is it that God don't answer prayers or what? Or God intentionally wished to frustrate him? Of course God would have complimented his efforts if he had done the right things. God can only complement our efforts but can never make the efforts for us.

The reason was clear; this man spent most of his life time wishing and praying, but forgot to work towards it. Prayer can never put food on your table but little prayer and little work can. Are you still wishing that God will prepare a paradise one day and ask you to walk in?

Thomas Edison made good summary of it *"Opportunity is missed by most people because it is dressed in overall and looks like work."*

EARLY STRIKE

Any man who spends 50% of his life sleeping, will spend 50%

of it suffering.

It is not all about postponing a problem. Postponing it will never bring an answer or solve it, it will remain there and the more confused you get. You don't live it for tomorrow or say that tomorrow will come. Yes tomorrow will come, but do you know whether you will come with tomorrow or you are going to pass away with before tomorrow.

Not everything needs slept over? I wrote in the previous chapters that one should like one's everyday life, as though one is dying the next day. When one is not conscious of today, one can never be anxious of tomorrow. And that is of course the hope of a better tomorrow which comes from our actions today. The hope of a better future restructures the life of a man. When one does not hope for a better future, one's present will crumble, because one wouldn't be easily moved.

If you don't place your eye on a vision you might easily be caught by a distraction.

It is either you fight for the name God gave you, or you will settle for the name the world will give you. It is either you bear a success or you bear a failure. All these things are true but a crumbled today hardly makes a humble tomorrow and one barely become what one is not. The early you strike the better it get.

Most time things appear to be true, but the truth. It appears to be a problem, but not that it can never be solved. You can appear to be empty but not empty.

It is time for us to understand that our courage is not far as we think and our doubt not nearer than we fear. Always get the right information and believe in your actions, because it takes a good formation to make a good foundation.

AND THE QUESTIONS

I gain strength by sharing my weakness.

My weakness might be your strength and your weakness my strength. Either way, we strengthen ourselves. In life, there are people who are suffering for losses. There are people who are recovering from losses and there are people enjoying their profits.

100% of all the questions any man ever can ask has been answered, but 50% of these answered questions has never been asked.

Do you want to be great? Yes! You can do. Do you want to be a failure? Yes! You can, it is possible. Whatever might be your doubt, there is a belief for it, whatever might be your fear, there is courage for it, whatever might be your regret, there can still be greatness, whatever might be your problem there is always a solution. Whatever might be your question, there is an answer for it but you have to dig deep.

If the answers are not in this book, it might be in other books written by other great men.

Many die asking answered questions.

Inconsiderate of the fact we live in sophisticated world, many still die in a world confiscated by ignorance. A world filled with darkness and negativity.

Most men are solutions to others, but problems to themselves. Most men are born to be answers, while they are questions.

Nothing can ever cause this problem, if not the mind confiscated by impossibilities.

You have abilities, but believe in disabilities, you can help others, but can't help yourself. You solve people's problems, but beg for solutions. You are the only person that can help yourself. Yes, because the best advice one can ever receive, is the advice one gives one self. Stop searching, start acting, stop looking, and start using your ideas.

Sometimes we need to take a step, other than receiving courageous advices.

CHAPTER EIGHT

Fight

"There are no limitation to the mind except those we acknowledge." – Napoleon Hill

According to Napoleon Hill whatever you acknowledge remains with you and that is what actually limits you. Explaining this, you actually limit yourself when you acknowledge the things that limit. You can make yourself unstoppable when you embrace the positive factors. The thing that limits are things that stand between you and your success; the doubt that discourages you, the fear that makes you scared, the mountains that makes you small.

If doubt can stop you, then you have to fight it. When doubt tells you can't do it, believe that you are the only one to determine that. Understand that it is a decision that you will have to make. When doubt tells you that many people have gone there and never lived, believe you are going there to survive and if doubt tells you that you have failed before, then believe that you are going to succeed now.

If doubt says that your chances of failing supersede your chances of succeeding; then believe you are going to maximize your chances of succeeding. If doubt tells you that you are going to die in pursuit of your purpose then you should understand that many die doing nothing, while some die doing some, so it is better you die, knowing that you died doing something. If doubt tells you that you are disfigured, then you might be, but not inferior and that shouldn't stop you from doing what you want.

If doubt tells you to quit, then it might be right, but not until you have succeeded. I don't know how it will come, but don't just stop doing something, don't stop saying something, don't stop fighting. I don't know how, but there is always going to be a way and the way is never to quit, never to quit believing.

If you can win the battle of the mind you are in control of your life. Remember we fail when we stop doing something and when you are doing something you can never lose the battle of your life. Many that have achieved greatness are those who stood for what they wanted. If you can stand alone on what you want even when there are reasons not to, then the world longs for you. The ordinary man gives just as needed while the outstanding man give more than enough, so the only factor that can make you outstanding is to give in more than enough to get you through the ordinary and give you what you desire.

I am so concerned about how you can live your live beyond doubt and limitation. Even though the odds are real, then you have to learn how to handle them. If you are feeling discouraged or positive, you might be right, but what determines how you feel is what you believe in and what you believe in is determined by what you think. If you are feeling discouraged you might just be right but you think you are.

Until you begin to see doubt as a wall between you and what you want, then you might never plan on knocking it off. Until you see doubt as the devil, you might never want to resist it. Just like the scripture acknowledge *"if you resist the devil, he will flee from you"* - **James 4:7.** If you resist the devil and he flies from you, then doubt, fear and lack of confidence can as well do the same.

You don't just have to accept whatever your mind gives you, you don't have to allow it determine what you get or how you live your life. The bible summaries it this way **Romans 12:2** *"Be not conformed to this world: but be* *ye transformed by the renewing of your mind that ye may prove what is that good, acceptable, and perfect, will of God".* You don't have to confirm to what doubt is saying; rather you keep fighting those negative thoughts by renewing your mind. There is something particularly meant for you; you don't have to accept anything.

AND FEELING IMPORTANT

While many have the problem of not doing what they want some can't just raise themselves beyond poor self-esteem. The problem of poor self-esteem is the problem of the mind. The problem of who you think you are and who you think you are not. The problem of not knowing what you want. The problem of looking down on yourself and comparing your success to other peoples. I am not writing now as a saint, but as once a victim.

As a matter of fact most problems people experience in different societies of the world are caused by poor self-esteem. Everybody just want to feel important, everybody wants to be the best no matter the cost, but no matter how hard they try, they keep feeling lost and empty, cheated and betrayed. It is really the problem of the mind. Being somebody? You are not somebody, you are nobody, you are just someone. It is wrong to think that you have to prove to people how important you are before you can feel important or approve yourself. Be yourself and interact normally with people. You don't have to compromise any of principle of your life just to be familiar or recognized by people or connect with people out of proving who you are.

Most times some people might just want others to approve things to them before they approve themselves and what if they don't approve you? You then go along hating yourself. They don't have to approve you before you approve yourself, do you know why? You are who you have become and one day, they will have to find out how important you are, definitely, they will come looking for you, then you will have to make your choice and that is what I call being important.

People naturally flow around those that are valuable, so what you need to do is to make yourself valuable by developing yourself. You are important if you think you are. It does matter if you are not being appreciated. Where you are at the moment does not matter, people may look down on you because they think you do not do things right but they are looking down on you, it doesn't really change who you are. You know who you are and that is what matters. Do not forget that there are people who are longing to have your kind of person around them.

Sometime ago, I found myself with some folks who I refused to see any significance in me no matter how hard I try to get closer to them, they never seem to relate with me. Out of curiosity I inquire from one of them why they don't want to be friendly with me, he told me that my life style seems to be exposed and more civilized, so they don't find it comfortable being around me.

As you can see, I was even different and important than I ever thought. From that day, I have never felt more important than ever. We feel inferior when we fail to appreciate ourselves. Appreciate who you are and what you have become then you will see how important you are. When you build your life on what people feel, then you might not actually live your life.

Like I wrote before the cause of poor self-esteem is as a result of how our minds work. You are the way you think you are. If you feel and think you are outstanding, and nobody makes you feel that way, do not think you are not irrespective of any reaction. We only build on a pre-determined mind-set and that is what brings us down. When someone wants to make you feel inferior and you fall for it, you didn't just started feeling inferior; right within. You are the one who felt empty and gave in to the effect of the wrong affirmation that you are not the right person. That means, you already feel that you are not the right person before they tell you. This is caused by lack of knowledge about oneself. You spend less time with yourself than you spend with others. You know others more than you know yourself.

Spend time with yourself, learn how to ward-off criticism, learn your weakness and your strength. Know yourself better, and when the guy comes around and tells you what he feels about you, you already know you are not that kind of person and you wouldn't fall for it. Most people will criticize you just because they can't become who you are no matter how they try. So they just want to change your perspective about yourself, so that you will stop believing in yourself and end up like them. Infact, if people should make me understand who I am, then something is wrong with me, because they can't tell me exactly all I need to know about myself.

You are second to none, and first to all. This is not pride, this is good self-image. It becomes bad when it gets into the way you relate with people. You are whatever you can become and whatever you are not you can't become. Have every reason to believe in yourself. If people say you are outstanding you should know that. If you can create a mental picture of yourself then forget about what the physical feature is saying in view of the fact that you already know yourself. Doubt whatever you can, but don't doubt yourself. You have to understand that you can never be what they say you are unless you want to, and you can ever be what you say you are unless you don't want.

Become the picture you want people to see not the feature they want you to have. If you are not just what they want you to be that's means that's not what you are meant to be. Your life is a race for you to run not to game for people to play. Take responsibility for your life because the way you end it is your doing.

You must be able to differentiate between what you want and what people want from you. Remember if you fail, you will be held responsible. People want many things and what you can't give them, you don't have. People love many things and what they can't get from you, you can't give them. If you want to offer them everything, then you will have to be many things.

If what they desire, you don't have that might mean that you have a desire and it should make the first order. You can be greater than what people think you are, but you never be greater than what you think you are.

If people can't believe in you, that indicate that they can't see what you are seeing, because if they can see what you are seeing; they won't have to believe in you they will depend on you! Those who can't make themselves happy will always make others believe that the world is miserable. Those who can't climb to top will always want companions at the bottom.

Don't allow anybody talk you out of what you want or be caught up in the misery people created in their lives out of their mistakes. Don't allow people make out of your life what they couldn't make out of themselves. This is your life and you have to take charge of it. Let you desire determine your want and let your want determine your action. Don't abandon your own life for someone else or allow someone else take control of it.

God has placed a passion in you and when you neglect it, you are neglecting God. You have to let the world see what you've got, they are dying for it. Challenge the next guy to take control of his life and forget about yours. I believe that human beings can achieve anything, and you can if you don't live your life depending on others. When people approve you and you have not approved yourself, you can achieve little.

I am willing to see you move out of that unfertile zone of your life that cripples your productivity and render you empty. Am willing to see you create out more out of your life and feel important. People can tell you a lot of things but what you accept becomes your believe. If you accept that you inferior, it is a personal decision not what you heard others say. Just like a man pointed out *"No man can make you feel inferior without your permission."* The negative things people say can't get to you if don't permit it.

Look at the things that are influencing your life: they are just they things you have built around your life. They things you approved to be right, they things you have reckoned with, they things you have believed in. when we change they thing we build around ourselves we change the things we get.

We can hardly surpass our believe because it is believe that triggers conviction. The only man who doesn't have a talent, is a man who hasn't discovered. So if you are still feeling empty, try to discover what you have and live your life to its peak.

CHAPTER NINE

The Impact

"There is nothing either good or bad but thinking makes it so".
– Shakespeare

One of the greatest achievements is the achievement of a positive mind, because every other achievement begins with it. The cause of our failure in life is not problem or poverty, for men succeed in the mist of problem and poverty and men fail in the mist of solution and abundance. The cause of failure is not problem or poverty, it is something that can be devastating and problematic when neglected – it is our mind.

When the environment within is damaged, the environment outside feels the impact. Just as you can never change a bad situation by wishing it were the opposite, in the same way you cannot change your situation by wishing it were better. But you can by falling in love with it and be committed to changing it. By changing your mind towards it, by making it look better even though it were worse.

A lot of people may try to ask why there are rich and poor people, some have tried to question why the rich struggles every day to remain at the top, while the poor struggles to get to the top. These questions are questions that may not have the answers we really need except we decide to see things differently. The world of success is filled up with failures and the world of failure is filled up with success.

Yes, the world of success is filled up with men who failed and succeeded by trying and the world of failures is filled up with men who once succeeded, failed and failed to try. This has just being the problem and we need to deal with it.

The easiest way to work it out in life is to have a before-success vision that tells you that you are there already and an after-success mentality that tells you that you have not gotten there.

Your solution to a problem today, can be a problem to a solution tomorrow.

Our life consist of what we have seen and what we are about to see, and when you think you have seen it all, you end up being with the one you have seen. Men don't like to fail and as a result they fear to fail; the fear of failure is the beginning of failure.

Fear prevents a man from navigating, from trying things that has a likelihood of success and failure. If the fear of failing was the mind set of great achievers, then they wouldn't have done anything, because to do it, a new way is always dark and crude. But they carved out what they wanted, with what they had. Just like Andre Gide said *"To discover new lands we must consent to loose sight of the shore,"* you can never see what you ought to be by looking at what has been.

A President of the United States of America, John Kennedy once concluded it this way *"We need men who can dream of the things that never were."* No success ever presents itself at the beginning, but when we dig deep, success will definitely surface.

You have to believe that you will succeed, not that you might succeed. In every fear lies courage. In every impossibility lies possibility, in every disability lies an ability. In every invention lies innovation, but it all depends on the way we see it and think about it. When you think about it negatively the possibility becomes impossible. Of course, there is nothing either good or bad but thinking makes it so.

Jack Welch stated it this way *"innovations comes from*

seeing the same old things a little differently".

BELIEVE AND MORE

Your success in life mostly depends on two things; your mind and your action.

Believe in what you want and always go for what you believe in. *Whenever I believe that I can do it, I do it more than I believed.* That you are not doing it in a well-known way doesn't mean you can't do it better. There is nothing more to this than a particular solution will give you a particular answer and a different solution will give you a different answer.

Charles M. Schwab put it this way *"When a man has put a limit on what he will do he has put a limit on what he can do."* You can never limit yourself when you have never gotten to the limit of course; there are no limits. Where you call *'top'* in this day and age might be *'step'* to someone in time to come. Your conclusion today might be someone else's introduction tomorrow.

The difference between men is that, some men live to succeed while some live to make impact. Men succeed when the follow the normal way, procedure and direction, while men make impact when they follow the unusual way, unknown procedures and extraordinary direction. A man invented a clock and men were producing clocks, but a man invented a clock that can announce time on its own, and he was called great.

Making an impact may not give you much success, but it will give completeness and an indelible mark of greatness in the chronicles of men and that is what I call real success.

Just like Napoleon Hill once noted *"If you cannot do great things do small things in a great way."* To do it a little more differently, you have to think about what the world needs, not what they have seen, the world have seen many things, but not everything. The universe is made up of verses of investment by investors. What you have where you are might be needed by someone in another part of the world. You are the one who will make it happen, stop looking at God. In some portions of the scriptures, God clarified it that he is not the one and that you are.

He did clarified it when He said in the book of **3 John 1:2** *"**Beloved, I wish above all things that thou mayest proper…**"* and he also called us gods in the book of **Psalm 82:6**, *"**I have said, Ye are gods…**"*

Does it mean that we all must prosper and be great? No, what it means is that the power to be great and the power to make an impact is within us; it is in you and it is in me. He said he *"wished"* not we *"must"*. We can become great if we want and this should tell us the reason why there are failures and social nuisances wondering the street.

There are things that connect you to this world and there are things you must do to get connected. Just like Tao Tse Chung stated it *"See what connects you to the universe, not what separate you from it"*.

See what connects you to your greatness, not what separates you.

Take a look at the following sentences:

- Positive thinking connects you.

- Negative thinking separates you.

- Courage connects you.

- Fear separates you.

It is important for you to know the things that connect you to life and the things that separate you from life. And above all you need to develop your potential.

When doubt doubts your ability it becomes disability, when your doubt doubts possibility it become impossibility.

Your courage is not far as you think and your doubt not as nearer than you fear.

Shakespeare put it this way *"It becomes what it becomes when it becomes when you think that that is what it should be".* You are in a race, race it now or you will be erased from the race.

There is a story about a man who had spent most of his life a drunk. One day he met an evangelist who preached to him and converted him to Christ. He became committed and dominated almost all the groups and departments in the church. But something wouldn't allow him continue and this made the clergy in charge of his local church to walk up to him to talk to him about it. The clergy advised him not to continue, not because he desired not to continue, but because he was already old and weak. The old man on hearing this wept and replied *"Son, I never knew I was purposed to be in God's vineyard, who knows what I would have been now if I had known earlier."* He continued and said *"Son, I have wasted 77years of my life doing nothing, and have only spent 2 years of it doing something.*" Few months later, the old man died and he died at the age of 79.

Wow! Full of years, but lacked life, impact and purpose. I have never seen a man who died a shameful death while fulfilling his purpose in life, but I have seen a men who died a shameful death for not fulfilling their purpose in life.

You are the shame and the fame you can ever get to yourself.

CHAPTER TEN

The Little Habit of Success

"Interestingly enough, many of the characteristics we acquire are simply the result of bad habits. Fear is a habit, so are self-pity, defeat, anxiety, despair and hopelessness. Winning, griping and complaining are simply bad habits even being negative is a bad habit". – Zig Ziglar

Interestingly enough, it is the habit that inhabits our mind with fear, hope, self -confidence and despair. What we create inside creates us outside.

Becoming a positive thinker is a habit you need to start developing, and there is no other way than to start seeing things differently. It is never too late to become a positive thinker. Positive thinkers started as negative thinkers and great thinkers started just like you.

"It is not by the gray of the hair that one knows the age of the heart" - Edward Bulwer Cylton

You are as old as you think. You are as great as you think. I have come to discover that the scariest things on earth are the things we fear, not the things that are actually scary. So whenever you feel discouraged, check yourself.

You are not far from what you think and what you think is not far from you, and whatever you allow to take over your mind takes over your life. Just like the scripture noted in the book of Matthew 12:35 *"A good man out of the good treasures of the heart bringeth forth good things; and an evil man out of evil treasure bringeth forth evil things."* So your life is more to your mind, and the way your life is, is the way your mind is.

Your life is the picture of your mind and your mind is the future of your life. So for you to nurture a great future, then you have to restructure your mind and nurture a great thought. Your mind gets you 80 miles closer to your success or failure and your action gets you 100% to it. That is to say, your mind performs 80% of the task and your action 20% of it.

Determination begins from the mind as well as success and hardworking, so your action only performs a predestined instruction. No matter how encouraged the body might be, if the mind is discouraged, the energy gets misused.

So it is what you think, and this can tell you what makes these categories of people different as noted by Confucius *"The superior man thinks always of virtue, the common man thinks of comfort."* Can this really mean that it is all about the position in the mind and not the position outside the mind? If this be true, then every man's position in life can actually be judged by the position in his mind. That is, the way you are outside is the way you are inside.

You are not far from what you think, and what you think is not far from you.

Your problem can stop you and you can stop your problem, it depends on how you think about it. Some people have problems but create out opportunities with them, while some people have opportunities but create out problems with them. Just according to the Scripture in **2 Corinthians 8:11-12** *"Now therefore perform the doing of it that as there was a readiness to will, so there may be a performance also out of that which ye have"* and *"For if there be first a willing mind, it is accepted according to that a man hath and not according to that he hath not."*

In life, for you to get what you don't have, you have to use what you have, a kind gesture can do the job, a local musical drum, even a penny can, but it all depends on how positive the mind is.

I recently read a story about a man, named Robbie, who

offered a 20 year old student $3 to help her get home safely after night out. Ms Harrison-Bentzen was queuing up for the cash machine in Preston city center, England, in the early hours of 4th December, 2014, when she realized she had lost her bank card. Seeing her plight Robbie offered her $3 for a taxi.

Although she didn't take the money, but she set out to find out the man's identity and discovered that he had been homeless for several months.

She then decided to set up a Facebook and twitter account, as well as a fundraising page to try and help Robbie. Ms Harrison-Bentzen once said *"I didn't take the money but I was touched by such a kind gesture from a man who faces ignorance everyday. So I set on a mission to find this man, the more I spoke about him the more kind gestures I learnt about such as him returning wallets untouched to pedestrians and offering his scarf to keep people warm. That's when I decided to change Robbie's life and help him, as he has helped many others."* Stop thinking about what happened think about what to do about what happened. Your own solution might be something that you cannot even think that will ever solve your problem.

Your donation today can be your solution tomorrow.

There are histories yet to be created and there are things yet to be done. There are lies yet untold and there are truth yet to be heard, as foolish as it may sound that's just the truth.

CHAPTER ELEVEN

Change the Way You Think and Take Control of Your Life

Is either you make the world rich or you make the world sick

Your life is either a gift to the world or a problem to it. It is a gift when you choose to discover who you are and make others live because of you, and a problem when you just want to live like the average on the street who hardly knows what he wants, who freely accepts what becomes of him without objection.

The life of a man is just a bunch of his decisions overtime and every of his actions has a seed to plant in his destiny. Many believe that their destiny can be delayed but can never be changed, but they have changed their destinies without knowing it. And the man standing next to me exclaimed *"my destiny is in the hands of the lord", Lord give it to me."* Ignorance in action!

Many are just living in the darkness they created, how can someone believe that his destiny is still in the hands of the lord when He already said that whatever you can become He has already made you. In the scriptures, in the Book of **Jeremiah 1:5** God made a decisive statement concerning man *"before I formed thee in the belly I knew thee, and before thou camest forth out of the womb I sanctified thee, and ordained thee a prophet unto nations."* God said he *"ordained Jeremiah"*, not that he will ordain him in time to come or when he is matured. That means whatever Jeremiah can become has already been, it has already existed before he came into existence. So whatever you can become has already been.

God has already made you, not that he will make none give it to you. You already have it, you have been made already; you just have to become it. It's important that you understand that God has already made you but He can never make you become. You become it, if you want. A friend asked me *"is it that God created every man to succeed?"* and I replied *"do you think that God created any man to fail?"* Do you think that God created you to fail? Do you think that God created you to live a miserable life? Do you think that God created you to live your life in poverty? Do you think that He created you to fail? If you can be able to answer the above questions, then you will understand that God has a lot of role to play in your life but what becomes of you is your own doing.

God wants you to succeed in as much as he cannot force you to succeed. If you want to succeed He is there to help you, if you want to fail, He can never stop you. He wants you to succeed if you want to succeed and He does not want you to fail, but all these are the decisions and choices you make. I am so much interested in this, because many have forsaken the responsibilities of their lives to ignorance.

Let me put it clear, your destiny is what you want it to be. Regardless of what your calling might be you can become what you want to be. Mr. Gabriel, my mentor once told me that whatever a man thinks and imagines naturally becomes a reality. Do you think that God can ever want you to be limited? God doesn't want you to be stocked to that career, he doesn't want you to be one thing; He wants you to achieve many things.

So many that have been called into the ministry think it is all about preaching the Word of God; no God wants you to do more than that and as a matter of fact the greater you become the more higher the gospel goes. Is it actually God's plan for your life or are you living in your ignorance? Let's consider men that has ever achieved greatness, be it in business, politics or ministry. They weren't just tied down to a particular thing.

You can be destined or purposed for a particular thing but that doesn't stop you from achieving many other things. To summarize these all, you are more than anything you think you are.

You are just anything you think you can become. Our real destiny comes from what we want and our ability to serve God with it and impact the world. Many are in the place of their calling but lacks impact and fulfillment.

An English mini dictionary defines destiny as the hidden power believed to control future events; fate. This is just a perfect summary of what destiny is. It is just a hidden power that we have to control our future our life and what we want to achieve.

You are programmed to do many things and when you think you are just for one thing, you are limiting yourself. Do you think that there is a limit to what you can achieve? Do you think that you are limited? Myles Munroe, one of the greatest writers the world has ever known was a government worker, a businessman, a teacher, a pastor, an author, etc. Who do you think you cannot become? What do you think you are? What do you think you can not become? When you place a limit to what you can become you place a limit to what God can do. One of the American respected reverend and writer Robert H. Schuller once wrote, *"If you dream it, you can do it."*

Your destiny is what you choose to become, not what you would become. You may want many things but what come to us are the things we go for. What do you want? Go for them and they will become yours. Whatever you can become has already being, but the question is do you really know them? Do you really want them? Are you ready to go for them? Remember you have the hidden power to control your future, to alter for good or bad.

You are meant for many things including your purpose. Whatever you think might be your purpose can never define how great you can become or how you end your life. If this be true, then you are the one to make yourself what you want to be not even your purpose. Of course many have great purposes but live around like nothing. What you want is who you become.

You define what you want. Look around you. People are just what they desired. Don't be scared to step into it. Don't be scared whether you will succeed or fail. One thing you have to understand about failure or the fear of failing is that if failure were real it would have stopped many that succeed and if success wasn't real many wouldn't have succeeded. Just build your mind and stay positive about what you want and stay for as long as it can take. You are too great to settle for the ordinary. Enrich the world with what is on the inside.

CHAPTER TWELVE

Success Summary

"Every star is known to be a thinker, and every committed thinker is bound to be a star." - David Oyedepo

The difference between successful people and unsuccessful people is that successful people do not like doing what unsuccessful people do and unsuccessful people do not like doing what successful people do.

Really there are prices to pay and if you can't pay the price for success you can't enjoy the prize of success. If success comes by wishing for it, then we all will learn how to make wishes. But Success is a personal cross to anyone who desires it. Many people might help you on the way but you have to get there yourself.

In our personal journey to success; many people have a role to play, but we have the price to pay

The level of one's potential can never determine the level of one's success (*of course many have great potential, but die impotent*) but the level of one's determination.

Our actions and determination writes the stories we tell

the world about our self. Our potential can never do what *"hard work,"* determination and positive mind can do, and *"hard work"* determination and positive mind can never do what potential can do, but they work together to do what they can't do when not combined. If determination, hard work, positive mind, discipline and potential is the formula then you need to start trying out something.

"God give every bird its food but does not throw it into the net". - J.G Holland

It is either you watch people do it or people watch you do it. They things people have not done are they things you are about to do. *When we do what people think we cannot do, we make them see what they have not seen.*

When we do things people have not seen, we make them ask questions that has never been asked. In my life, I have come to discover that some people live to make histories, while some people live to tell them. That explains while everybody sees the vision, but few sees the reality.

If you can be able to fight without quitting try without stopping search without resting fly without perching believe without doubting then I see you succeeding without failing

It is in our best interest to know that we make our lives what it becomes.

CONCLUSION

No man has ever become great with a negative mind and no man has ever become a failure with a positive mind. Everyman is just a product of his mind. The real battle for greatness is the battle of the mind and any man who conquers the mind is in control of his life. But it is important to know that the battle of the mind is a life-long-term battle everyman would have to handle.

No man can completely get rid of it, but can completely take control of it. I have come to discover that men, who have ever achieved success, were not men who totally got rid of the fear of failure, but men who took control of it. Fear of failure is a natural companion to the dream of success, which tells us what will happen if we loose grip on the hope of success.

I want you to understand that no man has ever achieved success in the absence of fear. Right down within, there is always a little fear of doing the wrong thing and this helps us to take a clear and determined decision. The truth is that, none of us has ever in reality witnessed success before achieving it, but we visualize it, imagine it, dream it, sleep with it, wake up on it, believe it and thereby building the courage to take a step.

Every positive man believes and knows that there is always a challenge, pot-hole, difficulty, temporal dead-ends, artificial-end of the tunnels in every success journey but the truth is, no man can ever tell how it will come and that strikes out many out of their courage zone to start wondering whether they would succeed or not. So it is possible for you to feel encouraged today and shattered tomorrow.

You have not in reality being there before, so expect what you have not seen before. And if you think that it will be completely smooth, then you are out to have a great shutdown, because sometimes, it gets harder than you think. Most times, it will pull you through a lot before you get one thing done rightly.

Anything any man wishes to become, or achieve has ever being but we have to discover it, carve it out, strike into it, believe that it has been, nurture it, then follow it to see what it folds to become. And that explains why things that has never been in existence comes into existence. Right before the creation of things and up to this day, most of the things that have never existed are the things that are existing. Things become what they are, if we think and believe that is what they should be.

So the journey of success is a journey of a predestined end. Before any man succeeds, he has already succeeded. We just get to trail success we get to discover the trails, the paths, the strength and the stumbling blocks. The more higher the fears, the greater the success becomes.

If there is any greater thing man has ever done, I believe it is starting out on the journey of success. It is just like a man looking for a treasure without a treasure map, but completely believes that there is a treasure down the lane. And not too many can handle that, not too many can believe that they are success while struggling with a serious crash, not too many can see the light while living in darkness, not too many can see the top from the bottom.

One of the greatest watchword that has ever kept me going, is that I never started to fail, so whatsoever I see on my way to success is a burden I have resolved and chosen to bear and the path that I have decided to take. The difference between a failure and a success is that a failure wants to succeed, knows he can succeed but does not know that success can sometimes look like failure, and so gives up when the energy is burned out.

Can you stay longer than a failure?

Can you dig more dipper than a quitter?

Can you give more extra than the ordinary?

If you can, then that's what makes you different from a failure; that's what gets you what you want. If men that have failed knew that if they had stayed longer they would have succeeded, they would have done things more differently. What you need to do is to hang on here, even though you didn't succeed at least die trying and never forget that you never started to fail. A short life of success is better than a long life of failure.

ABOUT THE AUTHOR

Patrick Uchechukwu is a highly recognized life-changing inspirational speaker, a teacher, mentor, coach and author. His organizational has trained and empowered youths at different categories.

Patrick Uchechukwu is the founder of Thinkers' World Organization, a fast growing organization that trains leaders. Patrick's in-born gift and unique blend of intuition has influenced and given many people reason to live and take control of their lives.

ABOUT THE BOOK

Y ou are characterized by the power to form an idea of something in your mind. But it matters how you use your powers of conception, judgment or inference because what you put on your thinking cap.

In this exceptionally well-informed and life-giving masterpiece, Patrick Uchechukwu gives you what you need to constantly choose positive way of setting your brain to work in order to attract positive events and have the abundance of good things in your life.

This work of genius will not just boost your motivation, it will empower you to shine your beauty from within and live a beautiful life.

The knowledge, attitude and skills you need to become a positive thinker and stay happy are wrapped up in this package of extraordinary optimism and positivity.

This is your time to look on the bright side of life and feel on top of the world.

This book will teach you how to achieve more, live longer, fulfill a worthwhile positive need in this world and do things that are out of this world.

9 789785 033724